A Guide to Equine Nutrition

Keith Allison

VETERINARY ADVISER
Christopher Day MRCVS

J.A. Allen
London

Contents

1 The diet of the modern horse

The diet of the modern horse differs from his evolved physiological requirements in two important respects. First, many compounded feeds contain inappropriate raw materials, and secondly, modern pastures do not contain sufficient varieties of herbage. There is increasing debate about these issues and the health problems associated with them.

One of the drawbacks of the modern approach to nutrition is that the manufacturing industries and many research establishments produce a great deal of complicated information, which can confuse those without specialist knowledge. Ironically, the more the information, the more difficult it is for the consumer to make an informed choice of feeding stuffs.

The basic principles of feeding are relatively simple, and are based on management practices which have developed over many hundreds of years. Once these are understood, it is easier to make decisions about the types of feeding stuffs to use, and perhaps more importantly which to avoid.

Holistic principles

The advice given in this guide is based on the scientific principles of holism, published by the philosopher Jan Christian Smuts (1870–1950). It was developed from the fundamental principle of nature, which is the creation and maintenance of wholes, or complete biological systems. Disharmony of any part, no matter how small, has the potential to disrupt the integrity of the system.

The generic use of the word holistic describes a system of management which follows these general principles. Therefore we may describe any practice concerned with equine husbandry as being 'holistic' if it is designed to take account of the maintenance of the whole.

Problems associated with modern compound feeds

Many of the standards for equine feeding stuffs have been extrapolated from the agricultural industry, where the most important considerations are to convert the food into meat or milk as cheaply as possible. This approach is basically flawed. Not only are the principles inappropriate because of the physiological differences between the species, but there are concerns about the long-term safety for horses of some of the products used.

Many compounded concentrate feeds contain by-products such as sugars and other inappropriate raw materials. Most include a vitamin and mineral pre-mix pellet which may contain a high level of synthetic products. Some may even contain animal or fish by-products. Often these facts come to light when there is a health problem, as holistic veterinarians will always take diet into consideration as part of the therapy.

It is difficult for the horse owner to identify unsuitable products in ordinary feeding stuffs and supplements. This is because raw materials are not always declared in a way which makes their nature clear without specialist knowledge. For example, 'wheat feed' sounds like a perfectly wholesome raw material, but is in fact a by-product of flour milling, consisting mainly of fragments of the outer skins and particles of the grain. There are around 100 by-products listed in the Feeding Stuffs Regulations, available from other food processing industries worldwide. Many of these may be included in equine diets. Some are worse than others; however, most of them would not be chosen by the horse owner as suitable food.

In order to give the horse a diet which is closest to that which he has evolved to eat it is necessary to use up to thirty different ingredients to provide the proper levels of natural vitamins and other vital nutrients in the correct form. Some of the herbage necessary for a fully balanced ration is difficult to obtain.

The best way to feed the horse is to feed unadulterated 'straights', that is, uncompounded feeds such as oats and barley, together with a properly selected herbal mixture. However, this method is not always practical for the one horse owner.

Problems associated with modern pastures

The horse is a browsing animal and must receive a variety of herbage as part of his diet in order to maintain good health. Because of the use of chemicals and fertilisers in modern farming methods this variety is no longer available in English pastures. Only around one quarter of the species of herbage found in pastures at the beginning of the twentieth century are still found in modern pastures. The current increase in the sales of herbal products for horses is an indication that more owners are aware of this. Unfortunately many of these products are not formulated on holistic science and feeding the wrong varieties of herbs may compound the problem, rather than alleviating it.

A look at the physiology of the horse and the way he has developed is helpful in understanding his food requirements.

'Straights'

It should be noted that although the term 'straights' is normally applied to grain and other base materials, and is generally thought to mean fresh unadulterated raw materials, the definition used in the Feeding Stuffs Regulations 1991 is slightly different:

'Straight feeding stuff' means a vegetable or animal product in its natural state, fresh or preserved, and any product derived from the industrial processing thereof, and any single organic or inorganic substance, whether or not it contains any additive, intended as such for oral animal feeding.

2 Evolution

The horse pre-dates man as an inhabitor of the earth by about 50 million years. The first true horse seems from fossil evidence to have been 'Eohippus', the dawn horse, a small, fox-sized mammal which appeared in the Eocene period around 55 million years ago. This early ancestor of the modern horse had four functional toes on each fore foot and three on each rear. The feet were padded and were probably adapted for living on soft marshy ground. The molar teeth were low crowned and had six rigid points, or cusps; the general dentition was suited to browsing on soft succulent herbage and fruits. The animal's environment was probably forest, or similar areas, providing dense cover which would enable it to evade predators.

Eohippus was probably the first true horse. He was about the size of a fox and lived on marshy ground. He had splayed toes and ate a wide variety of herbage and fruits.

The next representative was 'Miohippus' or 'Mesohippus', still living in forest areas. He stood two feet high at the shoulder, and his feet had changed significantly, in that he now only had three toes on each foot.

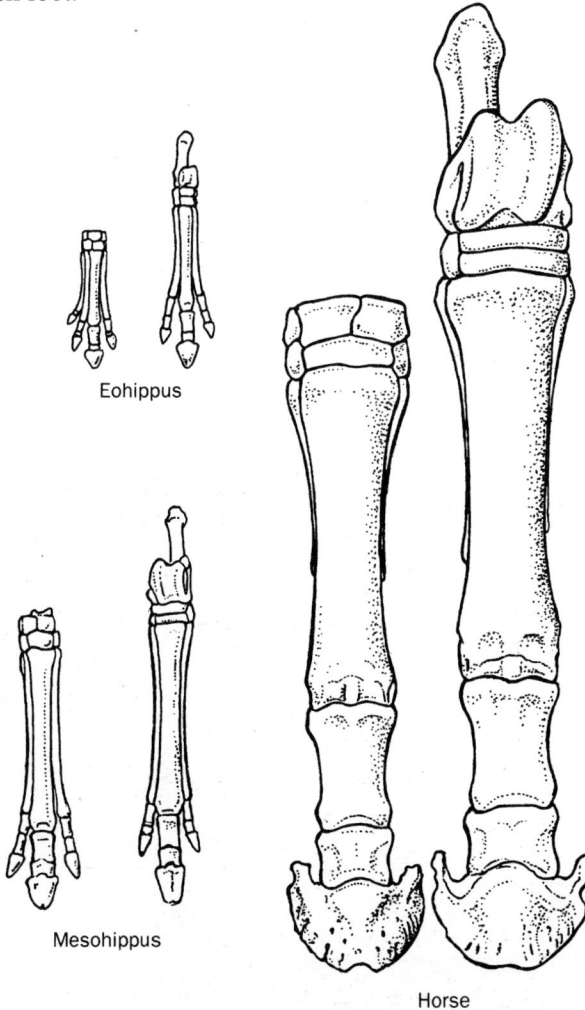

Eohippus

Mesohippus

Horse

The horse's feet (foreleg on the left of each pair, hind leg on the right) have changed along with his habitat. The single hoof of the modern horse is an adaptation of a former toe. Gradual movement from soft marshy ground on to the open plains brought a reduction in the number of toes as they were no longer needed to prevent sinking.

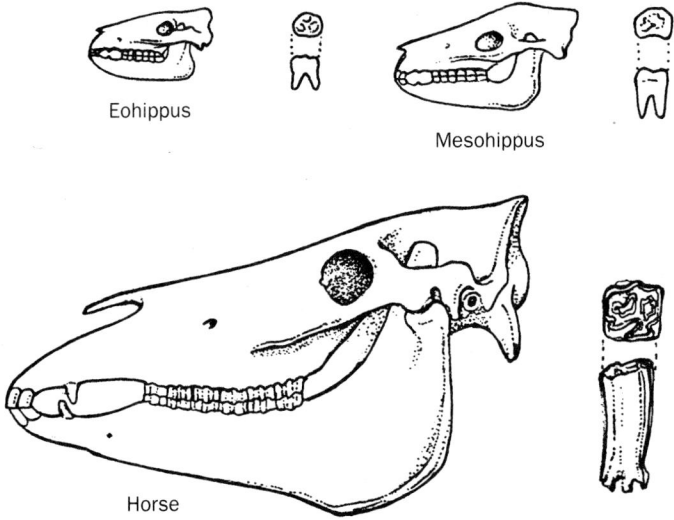

Eohippus

Mesohippus

Horse

As the horse evolved to eat tougher materials such as grass and herbage containing siliceous fibres, his dentition changed. The teeth (shown side view and top view) have developed very efficient grinding surfaces, and they continue to grow throughout life.

For reasons which are not clear, the horse gradually began to move from forest areas out into the open plains. The physiological adaptations to this environment produced important changes:

1. The digestive system was developed to derive optimum nutrition and health from a variety of high fibre, low energy plains grasses and herbage.
2. In common with other herbivores of the open plains, the horse became a 'trickle' feeder, large infrequent meals being inconsistent with a fast flight response from predators.

The diet of the modern horse is more often than not unsuited to these important physiological needs. As we have seen, the horse no longer has access to multi-species swards, and he is probably fed only two or three times a day. In addition, when the domesticated horse requires more energy for work it must be provided in the form of cereal grains or other concentrate feeds, to which his digestive system has not fully adapted (see p. 19).

3 The digestive system of the horse

The mouth

The digestive process starts in the mouth. As the food passes through the system it is broken down into a form which can be absorbed and utilised by the body.

The horse's sensitive lips with their attendant whiskers are very well adapted to locate, assess, and handle the herbage he wishes to eat. The sensitivity, mobility, and power of the lips is extraordinary. The front teeth, together with the lips and tongue, are used to get hold of the food and bring it into the mouth for grinding by the molars, or back teeth. The horse's powerful teeth are a reflection of the coarse grasses and herbage he has evolved to eat, which require considerable mastication in order to break down the tough siliceous fibres.

The constant process of grinding such food had the effect of wearing the teeth down. For this reason the horse has developed open-rooted teeth which continue to grow throughout his life. That the modern horse has to have his teeth regularly rasped is a reflection of the fact that modern food stuffs do not perform this function correctly. Proper maintenance of the teeth is vital to proper digestion.

The stomach

When the food reaches the stomach it is a semi-liquid mass. The digestion of proteins and fats begins here, through the introduction of powerful digestive juices secreted by the stomach. If the horse is fed a high proportion of concentrates, a significant amount of the processing will occur in the stomach. This must take place slowly. Because the stomach is comparatively small, serious problems will be caused if the horse is over-fed with concentrate feeds.

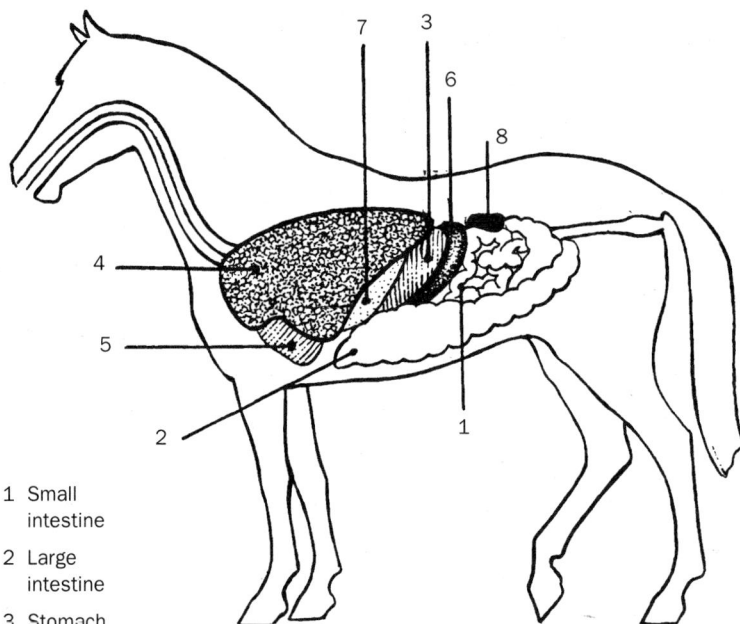

1 Small
  intestine

2 Large
  intestine

3 Stomach

4 Lungs

5 Heart   6 Spleen   7 Liver   8 Kidney

The main digestive organs seen in relation to the other internal organs.

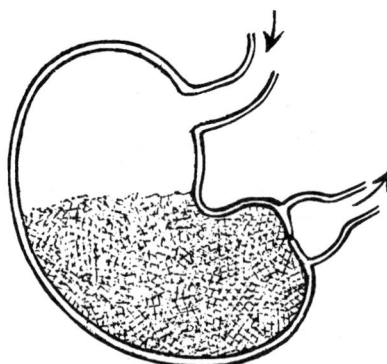

The horse's small stomach plays a relatively minor role in the digestion of the natural diet: low energy, high fibre foods are mainly digested in the large intestine. It is much more important in the digestion of high energy feeds, which should not be overfed as digestion must take place slowly.

The small and large intestines

Food enters the small intestine from the stomach. Here digestion of some parts of the food continues and the absorption of nutrients into the bloodstream begins. From here the food enters the large intestine which is the major organ for the digestion of roughage. The large intestine contains a large population of bacteria or 'gut flora' which are central to the proper digestion of cellulose, a major part of the horse's natural diet.

The goodness that the horse derives from the food depends intimately upon the composition of the gut flora. If it is disturbed the digestive process is impaired. Dramatic changes in the population associated with either a sudden change in diet or the long-term use of inappropriate ingredients can lead to allergy or acute poisoning. It can also cause serious problems such as colic and laminitis.

Longer-term problems associated with a disturbed gut flora are poor stamina, unthriftiness, or an unbalanced immune system leading to allergies or infections. Poor dentition can also cause a change in the gut flora.

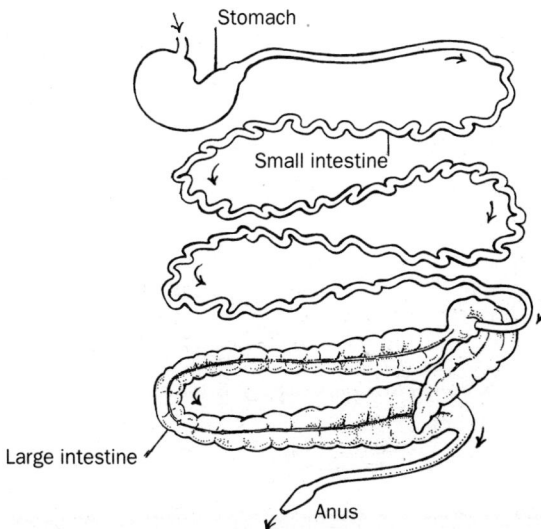

The main parts of the digestive system, laid out so all parts can be seen. The direction of the food is shown by the arrows.

4 Types of feeding stuffs

Only unadulterated raw materials should be used in horse feeds, and up to thirty are commonly included in holistic rations. Most modern compound feeds contain probably fewer than half that number. The contents of feeding stuffs and supplements must, by law, be declared on the product, but they are not always listed in a form which is easily understood. Always read the label and if the ingredients are not clear the free helpline run by the British Association of Holistic Nutrition and Medicine (BAHNM) will assist (see pp. 28, 31).

Roughage

Hay

Hay is dried grass and a good source of forage feed. Although hay forms a staple part of the diet of most horses, the quality is often not adequately considered. The quality of hay depends on five factors:

1. The grasses and herbage of which it is composed.
2. The soil on which it has been grown.
3. The time at which the grass has been cut.
4. The hay-making process itself.
5. The conditions of storage.

There are two types of hay available: meadow hay, which is cut from established pasture, and seed hay, which is grown especially for hay making. Seed hay is potentially higher in protein than meadow hay.

Hay should smell like new-mown grass. It should be dust free, and any which shows signs of mustiness should be rejected.

Alfalfa

Alfalfa (or lucerne) is being used increasingly as a horse feed. As a legume, it has a higher level of protein than most grasses. Unfortunately it is difficult to obtain without added sugars in the form of molasses, which is put in at the manufacturing stage to improve handling. Ideally sugars should not be added to horse feeds (see Molasses, p. 22).

Semi-wilted forage

This is grass which has been cut and compressed into plastic bags which are then heat sealed. The mild fermentation which goes on inside the bag effectively prevents any fungal spores from developing. This results in an almost dust-free product. It does not suit all horses, however, as diarrhoea has been observed. It should be noted that it is not the same as silage, which must never be fed to horses.

Straw

Horses with efficient digestion and good teeth may be given small quantities of wheat or barley straw; it is a good source of fibre. Because it has little nutrient value it should not be more than a small proportion of the total diet.

Herbs

The term herb may be applied to a wide range of plant species. The effects of most herbs on the body can vary dramatically according to the combination in which they are fed. Knowledge and experience of their actions are required in order to formulate effective and balanced holistic concentrate rations. Effective use of herbs requires many years training.

Although several concentrate feeds contain some of the fragrant varieties of herbs, these are designed to appeal to the owner, rather than for any known nutritional benefit. Feeds which claim to contain therapeutic herbage should not be used unless they are licensed holistic products under the BAHNM regulations (see p. 28).

Some herbs are very mild in their action, others very potent. At one end of the spectrum are complementary herbs which should be included in pastures for regular grazing as the horse requires them. In the middle range are herbs which can have a more specific physiological effect; these may be added to feeds for gentle nutritional therapy. Certain species are also used as a rich source of holistic vitamins and other micro-nutrients. At the other end of the spectrum are medicinal herbs which can be very potent, and must be used with extreme care. Many of these can be poisonous in unskilled hands.

Complementary herbage for pastures

The horse should have a variety of herbage as part of his diet. Because of the ecological changes which have taken place due to modern farming methods, it would be virtually impossible to provide all the varieties of herbage which were formerly found in pasture. A good start, however, would be to over-sow pastureland with the species of grasses as listed below. Unless holistic rations are being fed, other herbage would have to be provided from an external source. If herbal supplements are being used, care should be taken to feed the right species in the correct amounts.

A basic horse paddock mixture is:

Two varieties of perennial ryegrass (*Lolium perenne*): 50 per cent
Two varieties of creeping red fescue (*Festuca rubra*): 25 per cent
Crested dog's tail (*Cynosurus cristatus*): 10 per cent
Rough or smooth stalked meadow grass (*Poa trivialis* or *Poa pratensis*): 10 per cent
Wild white clover (*Trifolium repens*): 5 per cent

Other species, such as timothy or cocksfoot, may also be used. The following herbs are suitable for pastures: dandelion, chicory, yarrow, burnet, and wild garlic.

Therapeutic herbs

There is a multitude of different types of herbs available, some of which may be given to the horse on a regular basis, and others which should not; it is important to know the difference. It is also important to know the combined effect of different varieties.

Herbs which are useful for therapeutic purposes may be separated into different categories according to their actions. Most have several properties and they may be used in various

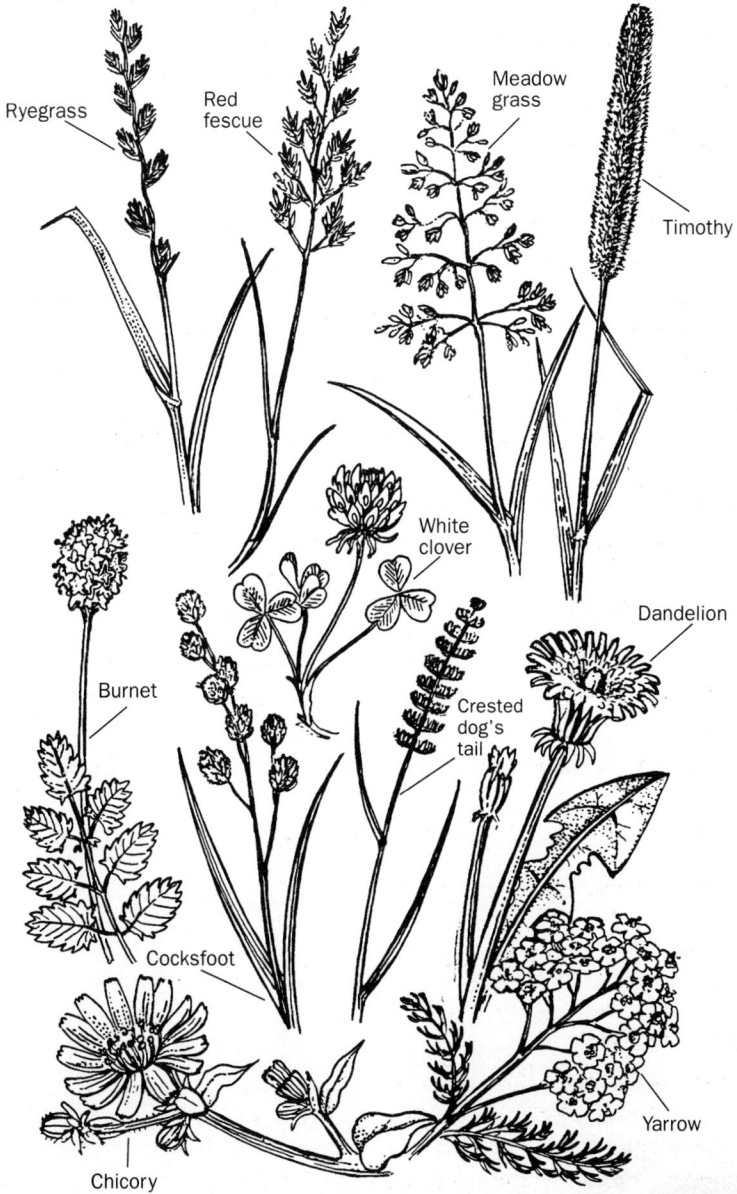

Ryegrass

Red fescue

Meadow grass

Timothy

White clover

Dandelion

Burnet

Crested dog's tail

Cocksfoot

Chicory

Yarrow

The horse should have access to a wide variety of grasses and herbage to maintain good health. Pastures may be over-sown with common species which the horse may eat as required.

combinations according to the effect required. There are over eighty different categories.

Alteratives: increase vitality and well-being. They are used to restore proper function and balance to the system.

Analgesics: pain relieving.

Anti-inflammatories: reduce inflammation.

Antilithics: dissolve stones or gravel in the kidneys.

Anti-virals: destroy or stop the growth of viral infection.

Astringents: have the effect of contracting tissue. They reduce discharge and secretions.

Bitters: act as a tonic for the system. Bitter in taste, they also stimulate the digestive system.

Demulcents: contain a large amount of mucilage, which soothes and calms irritated or inflamed mucous membranes.

Diuretics: increase the flow of fluid from the tissues.

Expectorants: loosen and help the body expel mucus from the respiratory tract.

Nervines: affect the nervous system. Various types may be used to either stimulate or calm the system.

Vulneraries: promote the healing of wounds and injuries.

Herbs can be most effective in treating various diseases and ailments. They are often used by holistic veterinarians, often in conjunction with other therapies such as acupuncture. The following are examples of therapeutic herbs in common use and some of their properties. Many more are available.

Celery seed (Apium graveolens): diuretic, good for the digestion, can relieve rheumatism.

Chamomile (Matricaria recutita): good for digestion, relaxant, can relieve rheumatism.

Comfrey (Symphytum officinale): promotes healing of skin wounds, soothes irritations.

Fenugreek (Trigonella foenum-graecum): lowers blood sugars, can relieve soreness and skin irritations.

Garlic (Allium sativum): reduces blood pressure and blood lipids, helps fight infection, helps digestion.

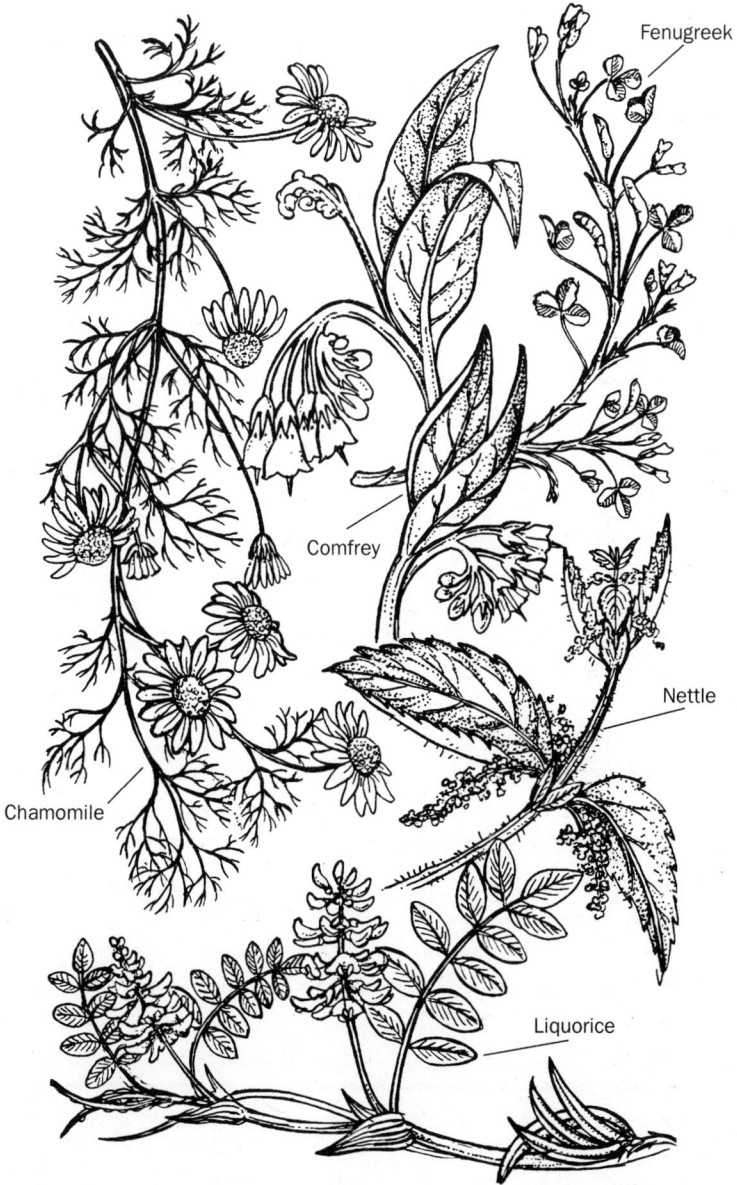

Fenugreek

Comfrey

Nettle

Chamomile

Liquorice

There is a wide variety of herbs which may be used for therapeutic purposes. Herbs should not be regarded as a cure all. They are most effective when used in conjunction with other therapies by holistic veterinarians.

Liquorice (*Glycyrrhiza glabra*): reduces respiratory congestion, reduces joint pain and stiffness, used in treatment of urinary problems.

Nettle (*Urtica dioica*): provides iron for the formation of red blood cells, lowers blood sugars.

Modern medicines derived from herbs

A substantial number of medicines available today are derived from plant, or herb, sources. These are powerful drugs, which must only be used by suitably qualified persons.

Aspirin: aspirin is a chemical imitation of salicin which is found in the bark of the white willow tree.

Reserpine: is a blood pressure medicine which is derived from an Asian shrub.

Ephedrine and pseudoephedrine: found in many cold remedies and derived from the ephedra plant.

Vincristine and vinblastine: both are derived from the rosy periwinkle tree, and are two of the most successful chemotherapeutic cancer treatments known.

Herbal supplements

The increasing demand for herbal supplements for horses has led to a number of unqualified people setting themselves up as experts, and in many cases giving veterinary advice. This not only puts the horse's health at risk, but it is against the law. If nutritional therapy is required it is in the best interests of the horse for a veterinary surgeon who practices holistic medicine to be consulted.

Many herbal additives available for horses are formulated with no scientific basis, or wrongly extrapolated from human herbals. They are being increasingly fed as routine supplements. It is commonly believed that because herbs are natural they are safe, but this is not always the case. Most of the herbal mixes sold do not give an exact indication of their contents, and problems may arise because of this and because of the cumulative effects of some of the ingredients. Therapeutic herbs, such as valerian, which is a powerful sedative, or devil's claw, a pain killer, are often used in proprietory herbal mixes. These should only be given under professional guidance. For more information on these matters contact the BAHNM (see pp. 28, 31).

Concentrate feeds

In order for the horse to be able to perform work, he must be provided with more concentrated forms of energy than his natural diet contains. The types of food required for this are digested in a different way from low energy forage. Therefore they must be of the right type and be fed with care.

Oats

Oats are the traditional grain food for horses, and they can be used as the total concentrate part of the feed. They may be associated with heating problems and need to be fed with care in this respect. Horses with good teeth can cope with them whole.

Barley

Barley is known as the fattening feed, as it contains a higher starch level than oats. It should be fed crimped and can be supplied as the total concentrate ration of the feed. Barley is sometimes extruded into 'nuggets', which process can destroy natural nutrients. It can also be micronised, which can have the same effect. Synthetic products are then added, the presence of which is indicated on the packaging in international units (I.U.). Molasses may also be added.

Maize

Maize is another grain with the reputation for being heating. Like other grains it may be fed whole to horses with sound teeth. When supplied as part of a compounded feed it is normally steamed and rolled. It is a good conditioning feed and can be used as a fair proportion of the concentrate ration.

Linseed

Linseed is a good source of protein, but it must be cooked before use to destroy poisonous enzymes. It produces a good coat condition, but should only be used as a very small part of the total feed. It can be laxative if used in large quantities.

Peas and beans

Peas and beans are often included in concentrate rations and are a good source of protein. They should only be used as a small proportion of the total ration.

Unmolassed chaff

Chaff made from hay or straw can be used to provide bulk for the diet and also to stop the horse bolting the food. It is often included in compounded rations and may also be bought separately.

How much to feed

How much to feed a horse must be calculated according to the weight of the animal and the amount of work being performed. Horses vary in the quantity and type of feed required and 'the eye of the master' is the best guide when making adjustments for individual animals. If holistic feeds are being given the horse will probably require slightly less compound feed for a given amount of work. This is because the food is being utilised more efficiently by the digestive system.

Generally a horse will eat about 2.5 per cent of its body weight per day, calculated on a dry matter basis. This is a rule of thumb – some horses need much more, others do well on less. Table 1 shows how to calculate the weight of the horse in order to work out the daily dry matter ration.

Having calculated the total amount of feed required per day the next step is to decide on the ratio between the roughage and the

Table 1.   Guide to approximate bodyweight

Height	Bodyweight in kg	(lb)
11 hands	120–260	(264–572)
12 hands	230–290	(506–638)
13 hands	290–350	(638–770)
14 hands	350–420	(770–924)
15 hands	420–520	(924–1144)
16 hands	500–600	(1100–1320)
17 hands	600–725	(1320–1595)

concentrate. This will depend on the amount of work being performed, as indicated in Table 2. Thus a Thoroughbred-type horse, of about 16 hh and weighing around 500 kg, might be fed according to Table 3.

Table 2. Forage–concentrate ratio for different work levels

Work level	Hay (%)	Concentrates (%)
Resting	100	0
Light work	75	25
Medium work	60	40
Hard work	40	60
Fast work	30	70

Table 3. Suggested feeding for a Thoroughbred-type horse (16 hh, 500 kg)

Work level	Hay kg	(lb)	Concentrates kg	(lb)
Resting	12.5	(28.0)	0	0
Light work	9.0	(21.0)	3.5	(7.0)
Medium work	7.5	(16.8)	5.0	(11.2)
Hard work	5.0	(11.2)	7.5	(16.8)
Fast work	3.75	(8.4)	8.75	(19.6)

Water

Around 60 per cent of the body tissue of the horse is water. A good proportion of this is provided as drinking water, the quality of which is often not given due consideration. The local water supply will vary according to the time of year. As well as being hard or soft, natural water supplies can be contaminated from many sources, such as farm chemicals, sewage, or industrial waste.

Tap water is a different matter, but it will still vary in chemical make-up depending on the time of year and the area of the country it comes from.

A constant supply of clean fresh water must always be available for the horse. Automatic drinkers are very useful and save a lot of time and effort, but, as with buckets, they must be kept clean and free from contamination.

5 Unsuitable raw materials

Molasses

Molasses is a sticky, thick black liquid which is a by-product of the sugar-refining industry. Together with other types of by-products from the same source, such as syrup, it is used in the majority of compound feeds. Ideally sugars should not be added because they can cause digestive and other problems (see p. 11). Some feeds contain up to 10 per cent of molasses.

Fish and animal by-products

The use of animal and fish by-products in horse feeds is not compatible with holistic principles. It is fundamentally wrong to give a herbivorous animal these products. The horse is simply not designed to eat or digest such foods. Many problems in herbivores are associated with the use of such products, for example, the disease BSE in cattle may have arisen in this way.

Sugar beet

Sugar beet is normally supplied as dried pellets or shreds, which must be soaked before use. Most contains a high proportion of added sugars, which ideally should not be fed to horses (see Molasses, above).

Other by-products

There are around 100 different by-products of the food manufacturing industry available for use in horse feeds. Such ingredients have been denatured through processing during the manufacture of other products.

Artificial or laboratory produced ingredients

Artificial vitamins and other micro-nutrients are commonly added to many horse feeds. This is done in order to fortify the product in an attempt to imitate the nutritional profile of a natural diet. Recommendations for the use of some of these products have been extrapolated from cattle science and their use in equines has not been adequately studied. Also, their use may compromise the immune system, in the same way as does any material which the body recognises as alien.

6 The Feeding Stuffs Regulations

The Feeding Stuffs Regulations 1991, with subsequent amendments, sets out the rules which must be followed by all manufacturers of animal feeding stuffs. The regulations are very complex and under constant review. Certain information which is thought to be of interest to the consumer must be given on all packaging, set out in a prescribed way in what is known as the 'statutory statement'. All raw materials used in the product must be declared, either listed individually or by using a generic term; synthetic vitamins must be declared as international units (I.U.). Because of the terminology used, it is sometimes difficult for those without specialist knowledge to make sense of this information. For example, it is not easy to identify by-products or synthetic ingredients. Responsible manufacturers will not try to conceal the contents of feeds; however, some are guarded when questioned about their products. There is a right to know exactly what is being fed to horses and the consumer should demand satisfaction. Further information on raw materials and associated matters may be obtained from the BAHNM (see pp. 28, 31).

Generic descriptions of ingredients

Under the Feeding Stuffs Regulations 1991, ingredients may be described by generic name. Some of these reflect the true nature of ingredients more than others.

For example:

Description	Definition
Cereal grains	The whole of the grain from all cereal types, regardless of their presentation, but from which no fraction other than the hulls has been removed.
Cereal grain products and by-products	Fractional products and by-products of cereal grains (other than oils).
Oils and fats	Oils and fats from animal and vegetable sources and their derivatives.
Products and by-products of tubers and roots	Products and by-products derived from tubers and roots (other than sugar beet)
Oil seed products and by-products	Fractional products and by-products of oil seeds and oil fruits (other than oils and fats).

Such descriptions are often used in order to conceal the true nature of raw materials. This is done for a variety of reasons: in feeds because the consumer may not approve of the material, and in supplements to try and prevent competition.

For example, animal fat in feeds may be described as 'oils and fats'; and such things as valerian, which is a sedative commonly used in herbal additives, may be innocently described as 'products and by-products of tubers or roots'.

Descriptions of individual ingredients

Of the 140 materials listed in the Feedings Stuffs Regulations, those described as 'meal', such as 'Wheat meal' or 'Barley meal', are almost pure cereals ground up straight from the field. Other products such as 'Flaked barley' are also pure. Most, however, are by-products, some commonly used, but whose name may be misleading.

For example:

Name of Material	Meaning
Wheat bran	By-product of flour manufacture, obtained from screened husked wheat or spelt. It consists principally of fragments of the outer skins and particles of grain from which the greater part of endosperm has been removed.
Wheat feed	By-product of flour manufacture, obtained from screened husked grains of wheat or spelt. It consists principally of fragments of the outer skins and of particles of grain from which less of the endosperm has been removed than in wheat bran.
Oat feed	By-product of oatmeal milling consisting of hulls, floury material, mealy matter and screen dust, all finely ground.
Rice bran	By-product of the second polishing of husked rice. It consists principally of particles of endosperm, of the aleurone layer and of the germ.
Maize gluten	Dried by-product of the manufacture of maize starch. It consists principally of gluten obtained during the separation of the starch.
Greaves	Product derived from the residues of the manufacture of tallow and other fats of animal origin.
Olive pulp meal	By-product of oil manufacture obtained by extraction from fruits of the olive tree, free as far as possible from fragments of stone.

7 The Medicines Act

Medical products

Any product sold to be given to the horse by mouth should be covered either by the Feeding Stuffs Regulations or the Medicines Act. Which legislation applies depends mainly on the claims that the manufacturer makes for the product. The legal definition is that if a 'medicinal claim' is made for the product it comes under the Medicines Act, but if there is no medicinal claim it comes under the Feeding Stuffs Regulations.

If a product comes under the Medicines Act, it must have a licence issued through the Veterinary Medicines Directorate. The product must satisfy strict conditions in the primary areas of quality, efficacy, and safety. These regulations are in place to protect the consumer and the animals in their charge.

Because many feed supplements are not officially recognised as medicinal products they automatically come under the Feeding Stuffs Regulations. This means that the raw materials used should be declared in the statutory statement as mentioned above, but terminology is frequently used which conceals the exact nature of the raw materials. The BAHNM can advise the consumer in these circumstances (see below).

8 The British Association of Holistic Nutrition and Medicine

Holistic feeding stuffs and supplements

Holistic practices and principles in nutrition and medicine were defined according to the principles of the scientific theory of holism, first published by Jan Christian Smuts.

Equine feeding stuffs and supplements licensed by the BAHNM as holistic products can be identified by a symbol which is carried on all packaging. Manufacturers must satisfy the BAHNM Certification Committee that products meet common standards. All raw materials and manufacturing methods must be approved, and the product must satisfy requirements in the primary areas of safety and quality.

The BAHNM takes advice from its own scientific and legal advisers, and collaborates with other organisations which have compatible aims and objectives. It also works with government departments involved with relevant legislation such as the Feeding Stuffs Regulations, the Medicines Act, and the Trade Descriptions Act.

The Association gives independent and impartial information through articles published in the equestrian press. It provides technical material and reference books, as well as a telephone helpline, for information on the following:

Health issues raised by inappropriate use of raw materials in feeding stuffs and supplements

Consumer rights

The Feeding Stuffs Regulations

The BAHNM regulations

Licensed holistic feeding stuffs and supplements

The Medicines Act

Licensed medical products

The Veterinary Surgeons Act and the law concerning the treatment of animals

9 The Veterinary Surgeons Act 1966

The Veterinary Surgeons Act 1966 makes it illegal for any person who is not a veterinary surgeon to treat or give advice for the treatment of any condition or disease of a horse. There are no exceptions to this rule. Those qualified in allied professions, such as nutritionists, dietitians, or nutritional therapists, must either work under the direct supervision of a veterinary surgeon, or, if acting alone, must not treat or give advice for the treatment of any condition or disease. The Act is quite clear.

Practising veterinary surgeons will indicate their membership of their governing body, the Royal College of Veterinary Surgeons, by the letters MRCVS or FRCVS after their name.

There are an increasing number of therapists offering their services in various capacities. It is the responsibility of the owner of the animal to check on their qualifications. Owners seeking help from those who are not veterinary surgeons are liable to prosecution under Animal Welfare Legislation if allowing, or seeking, such help causes an increase in or fails to delay suffering and pain.

The symbol of the British Association of Holistic Nutrition and Medicine which is carried on the packaging of licensed products.

10 The Trading Standards Department

The Trading Standards Department's duties are to improve and maintain standards of fair trading in terms of quality, quantity, safety and description.

The Department carries out its duties through inspection, sampling, testing, and investigation. It will enforce legislation by prosecution if necessary.

It also informs, advises and educates manufacturers, traders and consumers. The department works closely with government departments as well as outside bodies.

The department gives free, impartial and strictly confidential advice. There is never any reference made to the name of any individual making a complaint.

Useful addresses

ADAS (Food, Farming, Land and Leisure), *see local directories*

British Association of Holistic Nutrition and Medicine, 8 Borough Court Road, Hartley Wintney, Basingstoke, Hampshire RG27 8JA. Helpline tel. 01252 843282

British Association of Homoeopathic Veterinary Surgeons, Chinham House, Stanford in the Vale, Farringdon, Oxford SN7 8NQ

Royal College of Veterinary Surgeons, 32 Belgrave Square, London SW1X 8QP

Trading Standards Department, *see local directories*

British Library Cataloguing in Publication Data
A catalogue record for this book is available from the British Library.

ISBN 085 131 6352

Published in Great Britain in 1995 by

J. A. Allen & Company Limited
1 Lower Grosvenor Place, London SW1W 0EL

Typeset by Textype Typesetters, Cambridge
Printed in Great Britain by The Iceni Press, Fakenham, Norfolk